The World I Wrote

The World I Wrote

Violet Jessop

I'm tired of feeling alone, hurt, broken, dead inside, tired, like crying and giving up, angry, unsure, numb, and like my whole world has shattered.

I'm tired of pretending and saying I'm fine when all I feel like saying is that I'm miserable.

I'm tired of not sleeping, not being able to focus, and putting on a mask everywhere I go.

I'll be there for you when no one else is.

I'll be there to pick you up when you fall.

I'll be there to wipe away your tears.

I'll be there to fight your battles with you.

I'll be there when all is dark.

I'll be there to make you happy.

I'll be there when you need to feel loved.

I'll be there when you're hurt.

I'll be there when the world turns its back on you.

I'll be there when all hope is lost.

I'll be there…. No matter what.

Laying awake for your heart and mind are at war. Not finding any peace, and losing sleep. Not knowing what to do from the fear of what someone would do if they knew. Don't be afraid. You are not alone. I too, have sleeplessness from years of pain and hurt. But it will all be over soon. Don't worry.

She was proof
that even broken
people can smile.

Why worry about the future when it's not here yet? Why worry about the past when it's already over?

Don't let your past define who you are in the present. Don't let the scars of your life before now bring you down. You're stronger than that.

Don't think about all the pain and sorrow you've faced. Don't think about the many times your spirit and soul have died. You're smarter than that.

Don't think about the Hell you used to live in. Don't think about it, yet let your mind and soul grow from it and become stronger.

Forgive those who have hurt you, but don't forget what you learned from it, and never fall for the same thing again.

If you cannot forgive yourself and move on, you will never be able to really forgive someone else and move on with them.

I'm so exhausted, but my eyes won't shut
for an instant.

I feel like crying, vomiting, laughing, and
singing all at the same time.

I want to clean, but tear everything apart as
well.

I feel like collapsing to my knees in agony
and heartache, yet jumping for joy at the
same time.

What is this madness? Who is this broken
yet reborn person I see in the mirror? What
has she done to deserve all this confusion?

There is fire in my soul. The fire will not cease until it overcomes the pain, and replaces it with hope and love for myself and others.

There is fire in my veins. The fire will not grow until it succumbs to kindness. It is slowly suffocating so long as the anger grows.

There is fire in my eyes. The fire will not give up until it destroys all corruption and evil inside. As the fire grows, so does the goodness within.

Forever the fire burns…

Now that I'm alone, I am free.

No one weighing me down, happy as can be.

Now that I'm alone, I am myself.

No one tucking me away on a shelf.

Now that I'm alone, I am calm.

No one hammering nails into my palms.

Now that I am alone, I can think.

No one telling me when to blink.

Now that I'm alone, I can cry.

No one demanding I tell them why.

When the world brings you down, fight back. Anyone who tells you you're nothing was once told the same thing and couldn't fight back. Keep your ground, and always be willing to lend a hand.

Being there for someone is the best thing you can do. If you don't believe me, think of all your mother's done for you.

Someday you'll have
the courage to find
your own peace.

He broke my heart and soul.

But I still wanted him.

I never thought I'd lose him…

Until I did.

I finally fought back.

And now he's alone.

Regretting the day he lied to the one he thought he'd never lose…

Until he did.

I am strong.

I may be broken and damaged, but I am not weak. I have been through so much. More than you know. So don't call me weak unless you can go through the Hell I've been through and still be happy.

You lost your chance.

You claimed you wanted me,

but you betrayed me and denied it when I
caught you.

Everything we were is gone.

When you have no words, listen to the silence.

For it speaks.

It tells you the secrets of life, love, hope, and dreams.

It tells you what no one else will.

All you have to do is listen…

Why are you listening to the voices inside
your head that bring you down?

You're not the one at fault.

He was the one who stabbed you in the back
and left you to die.

Life is a circle. We live, we die.

But what do we do in the time that we live?

What will we be remembered for?

If we are to make the world a better place,
then why are we playing games and
gambling our lives away?

Get up and make a difference in the world.

Even in isolation you are not alone.

The birds, the trees, the grass. They are all with you.

No matter how alone you feel, you are not alone.

Just take a deep breath and smell the fresh air.

For others are there with you.

Look at me.

I am broken.

Yet, I can still smile and I am strong.

You don't control me anymore.

You walked away, and I found myself.

Now stay away.

I dream of a place where it's bright.

Of a place where no one suffers.

I dream of a place where I can rest.

Of a place where I don't feel alone.

I dream of a place where people are kind.

Of a place where it's happy.

I dream of a place where it's peaceful.

Of a place where no one's hurt.

I dream of a place where people forgive.

Of a place where it's pure.

I dream of a place where people care.

Of a place where it's calm.

I dream of a place where people love.

Of a place where loyalty exists…

Sometimes life isn't about living.

It's about surviving.

Sometimes surviving is about surviving.

It's about giving all you got.

Sometimes giving all you got isn't about giving all you got.

It's about trying.

Sometimes trying isn't about trying.

It's about being there.

Sometimes being there isn't about being there.

It's about caring.

Sometimes caring isn't about caring.

It's about living.

And living is life, so live life like you've got nothing to lose.

In my nightmares, the world is dark.

The world is full of pain.

In my nightmares, the children cry.

The parents have all died.

In my nightmares, the adults are heartless.

The children are left alone.

In my nightmares, the animals starve.

The humans feast.

In my nightmares, nothing makes sense.

No one can tell truth from lie.

In my nightmares, the plants die.

The creatures are killed.

In my nightmares, killing is a game.

Death is shown everywhere.

Sometimes people don't want to remember things. Or years. This year was one of those years.

It seems I needed a skin of titanium, and I only had steel.

Everything I cared about seemed to vanish, die, or break.

I was isolated.

It feels I've no tears left to cry, but instead a void inside me tearing at my soul.

I have never known

pain like this.

A part of me disappeared.

A part I may never get back.

A part that was the innocence within.

There comes a time in life that everyone feels like giving up.

The feeling of despair, hopelessness, and failure.

It's the feeling that kills inside, but no one knows what it is, or how to describe it.

This year I hid more pain, kept more secrets, and felt more alone than I knew was capable of myself.

The truth is, what doesn't kill you *doesn't* make you stronger.

It makes you weaker inside, stronger in appearance.

I am left in the dust of my own life speeding ahead of me.

As I try to catch up, I just fall more behind.

I am left behind until this journey ends.

This journey that may take years, but will come to an end someday. Someday....

When are you going to learn?

This is just painful. For everyone.

You need to get away.

You're just getting hurt.

Get out while you can.

I hope someday

you are able

to walk away

and finally be happy.

I told you everything.

You took it as ammo, and pulled the trigger.

I hope you're happy now that you're alone.

Why are you doing this to yourself?

You deserve so much better.

Get away from him.

He doesn't love you.

He just wants everything you'll give him.

Get out.

I'm glad I left you when I had the chance.

I should have listened to everyone who told me I deserved better, and never have trusted you.

You made me feel worthless.

Now you want me back, but you're too late.

I'm done with you.

You left me in the gutter to die but I got up and walked to peace, and now you're begging for me again, but why?

To see how worthless you can make me feel?

Good luck. I'm living a full life now.

I am proof
that broken people
can be happy.

Alone to my thoughts.

Nothing but silence.

And I find peace

When you left,

I didn't lose you.

I found myself,

and you lost me.

I am in pain,

yes,

but I am also in peace.

I laugh so much because I am broken.

Laughter puts me back together in the moment.

I never gave up.

I just moved on,

and found a better someone.

Someone worthy of my love.

Not a backstabber.

I have built a wall around my heart made of the pain you gave me.

Only a real man can climb the wall and get to my heart.

You said you were sorry,

but kept doing things to hurt me.

You said you were sorry,

but you had already broken me.

You broke me.

You were a demon in disguise.

I fell into your trap,

and it was too late when I got out.

I couldn't be fixed,

so I learned to live broken and shattered.

You made me seem like the demon you
were containing in yourself,

so when I left you, no one believed me when
I told them what had happened.

I was alone

I mistook you for an angel,

and all you ever were was a demon,

so now I'm gone.

Love should not be taken lightly.

You thought it was a feather while

I thought it was a brick.

Everyone hides something.

I hide pain.

You hide violence.

I began noticing things I never had before.

Things that horrified me, gave me nightmares, and made me jump at the smallest things.

This pain and fear was unusual.

It only came out at certain moments,

but when it did, there was no hiding it.

This required an insane amount of effort, but
with determination, I grew my skin of steel.
I grew layers of armor to protect myself
from the outside world, and the inside.

Years passed, and I began to be more and more broken. But no matter how deep it was, I couldn't show it.

I have to hide what I truly feel from the world, and hope I can get through the day without breaking down.

I always have my guard up for the unknown. What will happen if I do this?

Will it become a burden later on in life that everyone knows?

Will it make me vulnerable?

These are just a few of the many questions I ask myself when doing something.

Sometimes the pain people see
is only 10% of what we're really feeling.

Every day the pain gets worse.

There is no way to escape it, and yet, it's peaceful in a way.

I'm so used to it that I don't remember what it was like without it there.

I think if it ever went away, I'd feel terrified. Something inside would be empty.

Please don't do this again. You left.

Please keep it that way, I can't stand to have you leave me again. Either stay with me through it all, or don't ever come into my life. Please…

When I told you my secrets, I told you everything. It's such a shame you used them against me. I trusted you, but now you're alone in the dark while I'm off living my life.

You said you loved me. You said you couldn't imagine life without me. Is that what you're telling her now that you've left me? I hope you mean it for her sake.

You tell me you miss me, but do you really?

Did you miss me when we slowly deteriorated, or only now that I've moved on?

Why did you say you love me and then treat me worse than dirt?

Don't you know I poured my heart and soul into us?

And you just threw it away.

When I look in your eyes, I see who we used to be, and what you did to me.

You used to work magic on me,

but now,

you work it on her.

Love is being real, and truly there for someone no matter what.

Love is caring, laughing and crying with someone.

Love is reaching out and having faith in someone.

Love is shown in actions, not in words.

He was the wildfire, and I the rainstorm, but
I could only touch him once.

He was
the color
in my life.

I was a flame burning bright,

but you blew me out like a switch.

He was the water to tame the flame.

The well that never ran dry.

The river that carried so much.

He knows so much, yet is so naive.

He's all I've ever wanted.

But he'll never see me.

So I become the fire that needs tamed.

The bucket to draw the water from the well.

The sun in the drought.

The sand in the river.

I'll always see him, but he'll never be mine.

He'll always belong to the clouds in the lilac sky,

the earth beneath the red rockies,

and the stars in the indigo sky.

He will never be mine.

I wish I hadn't believed you
when you said you loved me.

The love you gave when you felt it was enough.

It was when you didn't feel it that you left me, and broke my mind.

You haunt my dreams and my reality.

You are the one I see in the crowd

that leaves me breathless.

And there is no escape.

One day, when we're older, we will find that we were not meant to be, and that you simply didn't see how much I was worth.

The silence haunts my mind.

The noise haunts my heart.

My mind searches for peace.

My heart searches for love.

My soul searches for happiness.

She is not someone to use.

She is a gem.

A diamond in the rough.

She carries the sword of determination

and the shield of survival.

She is you.

He withdrew himself from you,

and you reached out more.

He gave up on you,

and you tried harder.

It's time to move on from the boys who
don't know how to treat you.

I say I'm fine,

but if you look into my eyes,

you will see how broken I truly am.

She is the type of woman who is called
coldhearted and mean,

but if you really got to know her,

you would see that she is misunderstood.

That she is an angel in a human body.

I try to forget.

But my mind replays it.

I try to forget.

But my heart still aches from it.

I try to forget.

But my soul still loves it.

I try to forget.

But I'll always remember.

I still have sleepless nights from you.

You ruined me.

My heart, soul, and mind.

I thought you could change,

but I was wrong.

My heart will never be at rest.

You took it broken,

taped it back together,

and then shattered it into a million pieces.

"Will you ever love me the way I loved you?" I asked.

"No. But I do know one thing." He said.

"I will never love anyone more than I loved you."

I hope you find what you're looking for in her that I couldn't give to you.

You stabbed me in the back.

You broke me.

My love for you grows stronger every day.

I don't know what you've done,

but please keep doing it.

My love for you is like no other love I have felt.

I dream about you and us.

There is no sweeter thing than knowing you feel the same about me.

Some of us grew up too fast to be a child, and so we are known as the "born leaders".

In all reality, we are the ones who grew up broken, and so, we are the ones who are leaders because we understand things others do not. We are survivors.

You kept apologizing for the same thing you would repeatedly do to me,

so it came to a point where I wondered if you were really sorry,

or if you were just saying it to make me feel better.

She is the type of woman
who brought men to their knees
and women to their feet.

My love doesn't last forever.

It depends on how you treat me.

Love me as I love you, and

my love will never end.

Love comes at a price.

It seems someone always gets broken

from loving too much and not being loved
back.

It is in the moments we are alone

that we find ourselves,

and therefore, find peace.

He broke you.

But it is in the flames of pain that you are reborn.

The blizzard of hurt that you are covered.

The hurricane of fear that you are awoken once again.

And now, you are a diamond, and cannot be broken.

I was afraid.

I didn't want to hurt you, and so, I hurt
myself.

I shut myself from the world and hid.

But you found me and led me out of the
darkness.

And now I am free.

I was feared by many,

but loved my more.

I took my army and led them out of despair.

And now I am their leader.

They look to me for protection and survival.

You disguised hate as love,

and I fell for your trap.

But when I came back to reality,

I saw the truth.

Now you're alone,

Wishing you could have me once more.

She has the strength of 10,000 men,

A heart of gold, the mind of a fox,

The soul of God, and the will to survive.

She is you.

People say everything comes to an end.

But does your pain ever cease?

Do the memories of you breaking ever stop replaying?

Does your heartbreak ever subside?

I dream what I dream.

I cannot control my dreams, nor my reality.

Do not judge me based off what I cannot control.

She sleeps to forget the pain.

She cries to muffle the screams.

She smiles to hide herself.

She will never know the happy home,

The kind voices, the natural happiness.

All she knows is the screams and crying, the yelling and accusing, and the forced laughter and smiles.

She will forever be trapped in chaos.

She was a beautiful soul trapped in an ugly world.

The kind of woman with a warrior within.

She was the thunder in the storm, the whisper in the silence, the life in death, the peace in chaos, the light in the dark.

She is you.

She gave so much, yet received so little.

She loved unconditionally, but was only despised.

She was broken, she gave herself, loved too much, and waited too long.

And no one ever took what she gave, returned her love, or came for her.

She was broken.

She couldn't put her pain, grief, and sorrow
into words,

And so, she spoke with silence.

And that was enough.

There will come a time you will be able to
look him in the eye and say,

"this is not what I want."

Just take your time to heal.

The silence screams, and I find no peace.

The quiet is loud, and I am alone in chaos.

She was a normal woman…

Except that her will to survive was a diamond,

Her love was a volcano,

Her heart was a lion,

And her soul was an ocean.

She was a normal woman…

Except she wasn't.

You made me hate myself.

My heart aches for you, but you just don't care.

You'll wait for me until I get close,

Then you'll run away once more.

I thought I needed silence to find peace.

But the truth is the noise and chaos brought me more peace than the silence.

Darkness surrounds me.

Night engulfs me.

I am alone.

But it is in these moments that I am beautiful. Because I am free.

And it is in these moments that are the most memorable. Because they are real.

The wind in my hair, tangling it.

The frost on my nose, turning it numb.

The leaves falling around me, giving me a veil.

Hiding my identity.

Protecting my heart.

This is me. A young girl who knows true pain. A girl who is broken. A girl who finds trouble smiling. This is a girl who people fear when she shows her feelings. A girl who puts a mask on every day. This is a girl who doesn't need to be told she's beautiful, but instead that she's loved. A girl who loved too much and got demolished. This is a girl who is broken, but strong. A girl who has withstood so much, yet never given up. A girl who hides her feelings except through music, art, and writing. This is a girl who gets made fun of for her differences. A girl who stands out in the crowd. A girl who is lonely. This is a girl who's writings terrify people, and make them think she's more than gone. She is not. She will push through and survive. She is a warrior. She is a diamond in the rough. This is me: a warrior. A survivor. A diamond. A fire.
Irreplaceable,